Camila Parente

Housework in practical guides to life

Camila Parente

Housework in practical guides to life

Manuals for Brazilian women - 1960

ScienciaScripts

Cover image: www.ingimage.com

This book is a translation from the original published under ISBN 978-3-330-20079-1.

Publisher:
Sciencia Scripts
is a trademark of
Dodo Books Indian Ocean Ltd. and OmniScriptum S.R.L publishing group

120 High Road, East Finchley, London, N2 9ED, United Kingdom
Str. Armeneasca 28/1, office 1, Chisinau MD-2012, Republic of Moldova, Europe
Printed at: see last page
ISBN: 978-620-8-27332-3

Index

Introduction

The main objective of this research is to develop a study on the understanding of the behavioral manuals/guides *Biblioteca do Lar and Dicas e Conselhos Praticos para o Lar* and the magazine *O Livro do Lar,* on the perception of domestic work in Brazilian society in the 1960s.

To this end, attention is paid to the modernization of the housewife and domestic work and the emphasis on time saving, utility and domestic economy, so that the housewife becomes more practical and efficient. The question is: what is the proposed profile of the ideal housewife? Was there an idea of division of domestic labor intended for the home environment? How is home economics presented to housewives? What is meant by "modernity" from the point of view of the guides?

In the second half of the 20th century there were changes that had a major impact on Brazilian society, such as the rise of the middle class, urban growth and industrialization. At the same time, there were changes in the daily lives of men and women, such as greater contact and coexistence between both sexes, greater freedom in the relationship between parents and children, due to the growing possibilities of entering educational and professional systems, leisure, access to information.

It's worth noting that during the 1960s, women were thought of as being at home, and their happiness was associated with marriage, motherhood and domestic chores. Domestic chores were of fundamental importance if a woman was to be considered a good housewife.

The question arises as to the implications of these daily activities for family relationships, especially between husband and wife. Would the woman be the only one involved in household chores or could she count on the help of her husband and children to carry them out?

The use of behavior manuals/guides as a source for historical research will also be discussed. The practical guides designed essentially for the female public, containing themes related to the domestic environment and relationships with the family and with oneself, present themselves as a source for the field of historical research aimed at analyzing the process of building the relationship between women and the home environment in the second half of the 20th century in Brazil. Reading them can help us understand the behaviors, values and education expected of women and men in Brazilian society at that time.

1 Spreading a lifestyle for housewives

Between the 1960s and 1980s, Brazil went through a period of civilian military dictatorship, which began with the intervention of 1964 and the consequent end of Joao Goulart's government[1] . According to Borges (2003), during this historical moment, the Armed Forms used means such as censorship, repression and state terrorism in order to maneuver civil society.

Almeida (1998) points out, however, that the "economic miracle" - a surge in the expansion of the Brazilian economy - which took place at the same time as the intensification of authoritarianism, expanded opportunities for occupations in the job market, the rise of middle sectors, the diversification and modernization of consumer society, and the concentration of income.

Prado (2003, p. 234) points out that the economic miracle was the product of a historical confluence, in which favorable external conditions reinforced the growth spaces opened up by the conservative reforms of Castello Branco's government, which could lead to an identification between the economic success of the 1960s and 1970s and the military regime; however, it is worth noting that income distribution during this period was not equitable.

The economic reforms of Castello Branco's government - which began in 1964 - aimed to contain the inflation rate that had been rising in Brazil since the early 1960s. In order to achieve this goal, the government's economic team proposed reforms to the tax system and wage policy, using as its main strategy the Government's Economic Action Plan (Paeg), which, in 1965 and 1966, had the main objective of accelerating the pace of economic development and halting inflation.

[1] Joao Goulart was president of Brazil from 1961 to 1964.

In this context, we can see the creation of the National Tax Code, the National Treasury Adjustable Bonds (ORTNs), incentives for exports, the reformulation of the Brazilian financial system, increased credit to the private sector and improved conditions for attracting foreign capital. Despite failing to control inflation, these institutional reforms helped to create a model for economic growth.

During this period, consumer goods and heavy industries became more important. At the same time, companies were set up in the production and service sectors, finance, commerce, services in general, and infrastructure development. The minimum wage helps to change consumption patterns, from the moment that workers are better able to access industrialized products, technologies and consumer goods.

Consumption, spurred on by new economic strategies in the 1960s, also sought to include women as an integral part of the consumer market, meeting the demands of the industrial sectors of beauty products, household goods, cleaning products, food and household appliances.

There was an attempt to form a link between women and the machine age (HIGONNET, 1991), in which there was an attempt to establish a relationship between the female sex and products from the consumer goods industry, in which the needs of both were emphasized: the products needed to be sold, and women had to change the way they dressed, behaved and carried out household chores, due to the social transformations they were experiencing. Thus, there was a quest to transform not only the environment, but also women's behavior. "Dynamism, mobility and efficiency became values to which women aspired" (HIGONNET, 1991, p. 407).

Advertising helped both to expand this consumer economy and to propagate new values for women, since the products offered by the consumer goods industry were sometimes more related to the benefit that their possession would bring to people - the satisfaction of the purchase, the leisure provided by a given product - than to their practical function.

According to Buitoni (1990), advertising has a great connection with the women's press, considering that the magazine can be understood as "a window, a showcase" in which merchandise is displayed for readers, with the aim of instilling in them an interest in buying. The act of leafing through a magazine, in addition to providing contact with information and a sense of pleasure, also encourages consumption: "In magazines, goods are advertised with the aim of creating or reinforcing consumption habits: advertising is more timeless." (BUITONI, 1990, p. 18).

Mira (2001, p. 13) points out that in the 1960s the modernization of Brazilian society led to the transformation of sectors of cultural production, resulting in "the expansion of its production, technical evolution, professionalization and rationalization, with a view to the consumer market that was being formed thanks to the broader processes of industrialization and urbanization".

The entrepreneurial dimension of the press became clearer during the 20th century, when it was possible to see, at the same time, that products aimed at women were becoming a profitable sector. The magazine, which can also be understood as a commodity, had to show in all its characteristics - both its size and its content - its power to interest readers, to satisfy their needs as potential consumers; hence the importance of research to define the target audience and seek advertisers for specialized products for each need.

> Especially since the last three decades of the twentieth century, the logic of the market has come to view women as segmented and plural subjects, who make up growing portions of the workforce, draw horizons other than marriage and motherhood and cultivate new consumer habits. (LUCA, 2012, p. 458)

During the 1960s, the good housewife had to be economical,

creative, plan the household budget, provide good leisure for her children and husband, not bore the man and guarantee him a pleasant and serene space. These observations are found in women's guides and magazines, which sought to disseminate to their readers ways of acting, ways of behaving and ways of thinking that were in line with what they proposed.

It is worth noting, however, that during this period, despite the idealization of women as good mothers, wives and housewives, there was also a simultaneous struggle by women to win rights concerning sexuality, the body, violence against women and work issues - which was also seen at the end of the 19th century, focusing on social and political rights.

Pedro (2012), referring to feminism in Brazil between 1960 and 1980, observes that there were women who didn't like being associated with the term "feminist" because of the stereotypes that had been created around this word - they preferred to associate themselves with the Women's Liberation Movement. The term "feminist" was associated with homosexuality, characteristics considered masculine, resentment and bitterness. "Defining oneself as a feminist in Brazil was a big risk." (PEDRO, 2012, p. 240).

In addition to some women, certain media outlets, such as women's magazines, were also wary of using the term "feminist"; they were afraid of being identified in this way and losing their readership, losing advertisers and receiving a lot of criticism. However, this did not prevent feminist ideas from appearing in their content[2] . As Mira (2001, p. 133) points out, "[In the 1960s and 1970s] the new women's magazines were interpreting feminism in their own way and translating it for a mass of readers who were not directly involved with the movement, but who were affected by the changes in the condition of women [...]".

[2] One example is Carmen da Silva's articles in the section The Art of Being a Woman (19631985), in Claudia magazine.

As Lipovetsky (1997, p. 203) teaches, the model of the housewife that places women's tasks on a pedestal, that idealizes the wife-mother-domestic triad, who dedicates her life to the children and the happiness of the family, was already in force in the 19th century. During the period between the two world wars, this stereotype of the housewife was hardly questioned, being magnified in newspapers, magazines, books, textbooks and official speeches.

The author points out that the ideal housewife model reached its peak in 1950. Women were seen as belonging to the domestic sphere, and their happiness was associated with caring for their children and husband. In this way, "[...] the wife-mother-housewife is not considered to be an abstract, autonomous individual, belonging to herself" (LIPOVETSKY, 1997, p. 205); she would always be at the service of the other (husband and children), providing them with comfort, love, entertainment, healthy and hygienic habits.

The women's press helped to disseminate what was valid or not in terms of representations of women. Marriage, motherhood and domestic chores were seen as the source of happiness for the female sex, and they were represented as fragile, naïve creatures. According to Higonnet (1991, p. 418), "the values exalted were domestic perfection, heterosexuality and the family".

> Readers are urged to improve their physical appearance, to express their individuality, to run their homes more efficiently, more economically and with more love, and to triumph over adversity. The reader of women's magazines is encouraged to master her personal situation - but not to question it (HIGONNET, 1991, p. 418).

Bassanezi (1996) points out that advertisements about the mother who cares about her children and family, the young woman who is looking for a loving relationship, the modern, simple and practical woman, have been in vogue since 1945. With the development of the consumer goods industry, the image of the modern, simple and practical woman gained momentum in the mid-1950s. This valorization of the modern woman, however, contrasts with the valorization of manual domestic tasks (e.g. making curtains and dresses), which were part of everyday domestic life at the time.

> [...] the invitation for the reader to be a woman "of tomorrow", to use household appliances, change the decoration of the house, get used to buying magazines, etc - a whole modern facade - does not threaten traditional gender attributions; this woman, for example, remains responsible for domestic chores. (BASSANEZI, 1996, p. 29-30)

It's worth noting, however, that devotion to family and marriage is not the main focus of the ideal housewife model of the mid-20th century - which doesn't mean that it has disappeared - whose image is also associated with seduction, consumer happiness and emancipation from traditional habits. Products from the consumer goods industry, such as household appliances, canned food, cleaning products and cosmetics, are shown in advertisements as the means for housewives to achieve freedom - is it?

The housewife of the mid-20th century could count on the "comforts" of a vacuum cleaner, washing machine, canned fruit, hairdryer and hard-wearing flooring to be more practical and efficient in carrying out her daily household chores, without neglecting her beauty and well-being. She was also responsible for making decisions about good household purchases and for finding ways to save time and effort.

> In fact, the housewife, as seen in the 19th and 20th centuries, is fundamentally associated with the principles of management, work and efficiency typical of the modern era. The tasks she is entrusted with bear witness to this; it is a question of rationally managing the home, of being economical and a good manager, of ensuring order and cleanliness in the home, of being the guardian of the family's health [...] (LIPOVETSKY, 1997, p. 208).

In this way, the housewife, understood in this way, is involved in a utilitarian and productive mission, since she is in charge of functions that society in the mid-20th century wanted, a priori and essentially related to the female sex: health, caring for the husband and children, domestic economy, cleaning the house, the well-being and harmony of the family, the moral education of the children.

According to Morin (2005, p. 145), despite women's achievements in the social, political, educational, economic and cultural fields (the right to vote, for example), bourgeois women have not been able to break away from their domestic role. Added to this is the model of the modern woman, which is also linked to seduction, a comfortable life and love.

2 Modernization of the housewife and domestic work

According to Buitoni (1990), needs were created with the rise of the middle class, urbanization and industrialization. In this sense, the home environment gained prominence. "Architecture, decoration and household utensils were consumer products that were promoted and encouraged by the women's press. Everything had the philosophy of the practical and the functional." (BUITONI, 1990, p. 22). Practicality and usefulness became prominent aspects of the home.

The interior of the home required special attention. The domestic space was associated with cleanliness, decoration, hygienic precepts, the use of household appliances and, at the same time, the need for women to use their time rationally in order to carry out household chores efficiently, to study Home Economics in order to better manage the home, and to plan daily activities.

The "comfort" spread through advertisements for industrialized products (household appliances and canned goods, for example) needed the "help" of aspects such as time-saving and utility in order to be "effective". Industrialization and the growth of advertising, in this sense, helped to spread the notion of utility, which permeated the advertisements printed in the magazines[3] of the women's press, stimulating the consumption of products related to the domestic sphere.

The women's press was committed to disseminating useful information for housewives, with a view to making everyday domestic life "easier", through articles containing tips on tidying up the house and preparing culinary recipes. "If women took care of the home, and home

---

[3] Duarte (2005) states that in Claudia magazine, advertising generally took up half of its publication with beauty products, clothing, household appliances, food, etc.

meant a whole lot of practical knowledge, it was natural that women's periodicals devoted a lot of space to advice, recipes and procedures." (BUITONI, 1990, p. 73).

The question of usefulness, as well as involving the "easier" performance of household chores, also has an impact on the[4] relationship between the women's press and its readers, since, as there was room in the magazines for advice on how to organize the household, it is often inferred that copies of the women's press were collected.

In the magazine *O Livro do Lar* it is possible to see how the notion of utility and the modernization of domestic work was propagated to the housewife. "*O Livro do Lar* was prepared by the Claudia magazine team and is an edition of Editora Abril" (O LIVRO DO LAR, 1965, p.3), from 1965, at the request of RINSO - a brand of washing powder - produced by Industrias Gessy Lever S.A.

Claudia magazine and Editora Abril were chosen because they were "highly specialized in women's issues" (O LIVRO DO LAR, 1965, p. 3). The women's issues found on the pages of *O Livro do Lar* - which had width and length measurements Smaller than a paperback, it covers the topics of home management, psychological advice, food care, children, etiquette, fashion, beauty and home decoration.

At this point, it's interesting to pause for a moment and give a summary of the magazine Claudia, published by Editora Abril, which was chosen to prepare *O Livro do Lar.* According to Duarte (2005), Claudia magazine's articles sought to emphasize and reaffirm the roles traditionally associated with women: wife, housewife and mother. In addition, responsibility for the organization of the home and the family was essential.

---

[4]It's important to bear in mind, as Bruschini (1990, p. 73-74) points out, that, at first, the aim of the women's press was purely cultural. Gradually, it became clear that buying a magazine, as well as being pleasurable, could also be useful and instructive.

The "Brazilian woman" identified with the wife who cherished her husband's happiness, the housewife who made an effort to make her home pleasant, harmonious and clean, the mother who dedicated herself to caring for her children, the woman who was willing to learn about the products of the consumer goods industry in order to have more "free time for herself" and her family and to be an efficient housewife.

At the same time, however, as it reinforced the image that women should essentially be concerned with caring for their husbands, children and the home, it was possible to find articles in Claudia by journalist Carmen da Silva that questioned the stereotypes established about women as perfect mothers, wives and housewives, kind, tolerant and resigned beings.

According to Luca (2012), the female press, even if it wasn't necessarily produced by women, was aimed at the female public. The articles in this press were characterized by covering topics that didn't need to be the order of the day, and that could be used again, such as fashion, beauty, home, cooking, childcare, behavioural advice (these topics never lose their relevance); which signals Weak temporal links between current affairs and the women's press - "'Current' here [in the women's press] is just a synonym for new, a mediator of novelties and not a moment in time" (BUITONI, 1990, p. 1314). The periodicity of the publication of the women's press could be weekly, fortnightly, monthly, for longer periods of time.

The women's press sought to arouse the interest of its readers by providing light, attractive and diverse material, which prioritized a colloquial tone in the language established with the readership - which suggested the closeness of a friend to give advice at all times.

> [...] the women's magazines of the 20th century were to continue the functions of the manuals and expand their audience. In their sections we find the materials of the manuals in homeopathic doses. The magazines, which were not disposable as they are today, were kept for

> consultation. The bound volumes of *Revista Feminina* were a good gift, since the precepts it disseminated had a lasting life, just like the manuals. (CARVALHO, 2008, p. 32)

Therefore, it is necessary to question the ways in which women were presented by this press and to understand its developments, in order to understand which models of women were being established, why these models needed to be made, and what position was adopted by the women's press and by women themselves.

Figure 1 - Cover of *The Home Book*

Source: The Home Book, 1965.

The Home Book was not intended to be sold, as it was designed "to be handled exclusively by you [the reader]" (O LIVRO DO LAR, 1965, p. 3), and the woman "will find in it a good friend" (O LIVRO DO LAR, 1965, p. 3). It contains "the best, most interesting and up-to-date information on women and the home", as well as tips on how to solve everyday problems in the domestic sphere.

As a "free offer of RINSO", the modernization of the housewife and domestic work can be seen in the tips for carrying out the domestic activity of washing clothes - it was advised that this domestic task should be carried out using RINSO, whether washing by hand or washing machine, because "remember that the manufacturers of the most famous machines recommend RINSO. Its purity and the ease with which it dissolves ensure that the machine works properly" (O LIVRO DO LAR, 1965, p. 8). Another important point that RINSO evokes for you is its reuse in household chores: the water that was used to wash the family's clothes can be used to wash the kitchen, the bathroom and the yard.

In this case, we can see the desire to modernize the housewife as soon as the industrialized product - RINSO washing powder - is introduced into women's daily lives. The advertising of industrialized products can be seen between the lines, when the qualities of RINSO are exalted (to describe it, nouns such as *purity* and *ease are used), as* well as combining the good functioning of the washing machine with the use of the aforementioned washing powder ("remember that the manufacturers of the most famous washing machines recommend RINSO. Its purity and the ease with which it dissolves ensure that the machine works properly"). It should also be noted that RINSO is not restricted to its function as a washing powder: it can be used in other areas of the household, making rooms (such as the kitchen, bathroom and backyard) cleaner, helping housewives to save on water and soap.

In this way, the modernization of the housewife and domestic work *in The Household Book can* be seen when it tries to include industrialized products (washing powder, washing machine) in everyday household chores. In addition, the aim is to teach the housewife *how, when* and *where to* use these products; thus serving as a kind of guide, showing the techniques necessary for women to be "modern" and "facilitate" the execution of daily activities in the domestic sphere.

It is interesting to note, however, the ambiguity surrounding the modern housewife profile that the women's press wanted to propagate to its readers, since, as Buitoni (1981) points out

> The reader thinks she is participating in modernity, when she is only helping to maintain the "status quo". Enjoying the signs of the new gives the illusion of sharing the standard of living of a highly developed country. It is equivalent to an initiation, the knowledge of a code, a ritual introduction (p. 133).

The process of modernization in Brazil affected all aspects of society, especially during the last four decades of the 20th century. The changes brought about by modernization, however, did not involve all areas equally, since some aspects remained unchanged. An example of this is the universality and persistence of a sexual division of labor, in which men are responsible for productive, income-generating activities carried out in the public sphere, and women for caring for the domestic sphere and the family - including attention to the physical and mental aspects of family members.

The rapid change involved in modernization helps to bring about a succession of new ideals, which show the subject in different ways of knowing himself and making his image known. The speed of the modernization process, in structural terms, as Figueira (1987) points out, means that there is the simultaneous existence of ideals and identities understood as "archaic" and "modern", in the same subject - and this characteristic is shown invisibly and/or unconsciously, where the "modern" is highlighted to the detriment of the "archaic".

Thus, the addition of the adjective "modern" does not significantly alter the images drawn around women, since, as Buitoni (1981) observes,

> The concrete change that women show in the social context is minimal, even those most exposed to the concepts conveyed by the media. And even the image presented by the women's press includes few elements

> of innovation. [...] It [the transformation of women's image] never goes beyond the limits of adapting to current norms. (BUITONI, 1981, p.133)

In relation to *The Home Book,* the "modern" sphere of the housewife is limited to the latest in industrialized products, increasingly confining women to the confines of the home. "Modern", in this case, consists of continuing with the same domestic behavior, with the addition of feeding the consumption of industrialized products offered to her in the pages of the women's press.

Regarding the notion of usefulness, *The Household Book* suggests ten commandments that the housewife should follow in order to keep the kitchen clean and organized. During and after carrying out each task (e.g. washing dishes, washing pans, washing the kitchen sink, tidying drawers and cupboards, cleaning the stove), maximum care and attention should be taken to leave everything in order and clean: "Adopt the motto: a place for everything and everything in its place." (THE HOME BOOK, 1965, p. 16)

A sort of "step-by-step" guide is given on how to do each of the household chores covered by the Ten Commandments correctly - which are: the dishes and glasses, the pots and pans, the kitchen sink, tidying the kitchen, the stove, the tiles, the cupboard doors, the order of the cupboards, the fridge, the cans and jars of food and spices.

There is also a list of basic materials so that housewives can equip their kitchens and better prepare their culinary recipes. Among the necessary items, one can see the inclusion (although not in the majority) of household appliances, such as an electric mixer, blender, meat grinder, pasta maker and pastry maker. The other products suggested can also be associated with the demands of the consumer goods industry for specialized products, such as molds (Pyrex or porcelain) of various sizes for pudding, cake, pie, pies; juicers for food (e.g. garlic, onions and potatoes), different types of knives (e.g. serrated bread knives, sharp knives for peeling vegetables, sharp knives for meat), complete cleaning equipment.

In addition to the ten commandments and the list of basic materials for equipping a kitchen, the "Small tips" section provides information on the characteristics (at the time of purchase) and the state of preservation (how to preserve it at home) required of fish so that it can be used in gastronomic recipes and does not compromise the family's health, and an indication of the dish corresponding to each type of fish; the characteristics (at the time of purchase) and the state of preservation (how to preserve it at home) required of poultry so that it can be used in gastronomic recipes, and an indication of the average cooking time required for each type of poultry; as well as information on the care needed to prepare vegetables, and tips for preparing beans.

> If you cook enough beans for several days and keep them in the fridge, unseasoned, to season only the amount to be consumed in one meal each day, they will always taste like fresh beans. However, if you have seasoned beans left over and you want to use them, boil them with a small piece of bay leaf before serving. The "stale" taste will disappear. (THE HOME BOOK, 1965, p.25)

According to Bruschini (1990), carrying out household chores took up all of a woman's time, including leisure and rest, since some tasks are understood to be centralized, non-extendable and cannot be delegated to someone else. The housewife, even if she is not physically at home, is aware of and keeps informed about the daily life of the house and the family, since she actively participates in formulating the domestic routine of the home, as well as knowing about the activities carried out by the other family members in the public sphere.

Women's daily lives[5] are permeated by a variety of domestic

---

[5]Bruschini (1990) points out that the coordination of household chores by the housewife "seems to be maintained even when she is not actually present in the house, since the wives who work outside the home are also informed about everything that goes on inside the house, making an additional effort to do so" (BRUSCHINI, 1990, p. 112). To find out more about the relationship

chores in the home, including cleaning the house and the furniture/utensils in it, taking care of food and personal hygiene and that of family members, and looking after the family, not only physically but also emotionally. The possibility of acquiring products from the consumer goods industry has not relieved women of the responsibility of carrying out domestic activities. It is interesting to bear in mind the notion that

> The purpose of repairing and maintaining the home and the equipment in it is to increase the time and quality of use of the goods that make up the family patrimony. The life and usefulness of the house, furniture and appliances are reduced or increased according to the way they are protected and repaired (BRUSCHINI, 1990, p. 108).

In this way, it is worth noting the distinction made by Bruschini (1990) between "natural time" and "rational time", in relation to time and the housewife, in the confines of the home, while carrying out domestic chores:

> [...] "natural time", [is] lived by women in domestic work, whose rhythm is given by the body and whose limit is tiredness, and "rational time", [is] defined by the rules of production; [...] [paying attention to] the difference between the time said, referred to in the discourse of the women themselves, which tries to fit into the logic of "rational time" and the observed time, which is contradictory to the first when measured by the observer. (p.43)

"Natural time" is the time of domestic work, and is determined by the rhythm of the woman's body and her availability to the family. It is important to bear in mind, however, that this "natural time" is also subject to alterations and limitations determined by "production time", "rational time", which is included in the domestic sphere through the other members of the family who are an integral part of the environment outside the home (children and school, husband and work), or by the woman herself when she participates in the labor market.

If, on the one hand, the housewife can set her own pace for

---

between women and domestic work, read BRUSCHINI, Maria Cristina Aranha. **Mulher, casa e famflia:** cotidiano nas camadas medias paulistas. Sao Paulo: Fundagao Carlos Chagas: Vertice, Editora Revista dos Tribunais, 1990.

carrying out household chores, without being subject to "production time", at the same time, she has to organize her own time according to the other members of the family who, in turn, are subject to the time determined outside the home.

In this sense, it's interesting to go back in time and look at Perrot's (2005) discussion of the relationship between women and machines in the 19th century. Referring to domestic work, the author points out that

> Mechanization reduces difficulty, frees up time [...] The vacuum cleaner, the firstborn of the electricity fairy, like Saint Michael the Archangel, destroys dust, the vehicle of tuberculosis. In the housewife's crusade against dirt, it is the most faithful ally. [...] Housework is now given the dignity of the "Arts", of which the woman is the ordainer. (PERROT, 2005, p. 225)

We can see the search for a connection between women and machines, in which there would be, among other "advantages", the benefit of saving time while doing household chores. "Every new machine given to women is presented as being part of a natural sequence of movements that require simple adaptation." (PERROT, 2005, p. 226).

It would be up to women to adapt to the use of machines in the workplace.

The mechanization allows the available bourgeois women to devote themselves to the culture of the body and the spirit, and the women of the people to produce more." (PERROT, 2005, p. 225). (PERROT, 2005, p. 225) - which does not mean obtaining free time to devote to herself, since the housewife's daily life, as Perrot (2005) and Bruschini (1990) point out, revolves around the needs of the other members of the family.

"Between the acquisition of goods on the market and their consumption by family members, a lot of work is needed." (BRUSCHINI, 1990, p. 109). Saving time was therefore of enormous importance to the housewife, since she had to divide her time between looking after the house and the family, and still have to look attractive to her husband. She had to know how to divide and organize her time throughout the day.

In *The Household Book,* it is possible to see how time saving was propagated to the housewife. In it, there is advice on how women should act in relation to food shopping and the distribution of household chores.

With regard to food shopping, in addition to indicating how the money should be used, it is also emphasized how often the housewife should leave the house for this purpose. It was suggested that purchases should not be made on credit, but in cash, as this would enable the housewife to choose the best supplier and the best nails. It is also indicated which groceries should be bought once at the beginning of the month, which should be checked two to three times a week, and which should be bought daily. At the same time, the importance of planning is emphasized so that the housewife or maid[6] doesn't leave the house all the time, "which would be a waste of time" (O LIVRO DO LAR, 1965, p. 6).

With regard to the distribution of household chores, *The Household Book* places the responsibility for household chores on the woman, regardless of whether or not she has a maid. It is recommended that a table be drawn up - each housewife adapts the suggested table according to her needs - with the distribution of chores throughout the day, week and month, "so that everything is done on time without rushing and without excessive fatigue" (O LIVRO DO LAR, 1965, p. 7).

Table 1 - Organization of household chores during the week

Day of the week	**Household chores**
Monday	Laundry
Tuesday	Ironing
Wednesday	General cleaning of bedrooms
Thursday	General cleaning of rooms

[6]*The Livro do Lar* presents the possibility of the housewife having a maid to do the household chores. However, this did not absolve the housewife of her responsibility to take care of the organization of the home.

Friday	General cleaning of the bathroom
Saturday	Cleaning the kitchen

Source: *The Home Book*

Mentioned division of household chores during the week and recommended to housewives as a solution to improve their domestic routine, tidying up the house and allowing them to rest with their loved ones on Sunday:

> That's it, my friend! Your house is perfectly clean and tidy and you don't feel tired because the cleaning and tidying has been done little by little without any fuss or fuss. All you need now is a quiet Sunday to spend with your loved ones. (THE HOME BOOK, 1965, p. 9)

Women should keep an eye on household chores, organizing and distributing them throughout the day, week and month, even if they have a maid: "If you have a maid, instruct her to follow this method so that she can do the work more perfectly and with less fatigue." (THE HOME BOOK, 1965, p. 9).

In this way, there was an effort to show housewives how to achieve the goal of looking after the house without "wasting time". The idea of saving time was used to make women give up "part" of their time to do household chores, with the "promise" that they would then have the option of setting aside time for themselves to do whatever they wanted - in other words, to do something that was seen as proper to the female sex, due to their kind, benevolent, tolerant and patient nature.

3 Practical tips and advice for the home

Chartier (2003) points out that reading can give rise to different meanings for those reading a particular book (for example), due to factors such as age, purpose and the expectations placed on the text. At the same time, the way in which the book reaches its reader also interferes with their way of understanding what is written there. Each reader expresses his or her own understanding of what has been written. Interpretations can be influenced by the content of the writing, the way it was shown to the reader, the meaning the writing has in a particular environment, the reader's life experiences, the reader's contact with other people - who, in turn, have other worldviews. In the same way, those responsible for creating, preparing, making and distributing/selling the writing also have various interpretations of what the final result of the text should be, and their opinions converge or diverge.

Taking the example of behavioral manuals aimed at women, it's interesting to ask: were they bought? Were they given? What is the purpose of these publications? What is the profile of the reader? Are those reading the guide interested in its content as a whole or only in specific parts, such as the tips for organizing the home?

These points help us to understand the importance of not thinking of reading as having a single meaning, since the same guide, in this case, can provoke different meanings in different people. It is therefore interesting to pay attention to the relationships that can be established around the same guide, such as: reader and guide, author and guide, reader and author, author and author, reader and reader.

> On the one hand, reading is a creative practice, an activity that produces unique meanings, meanings that are in no way reducible to the intentions of the authors of texts or book publishers [...] On the other hand, the reader is always thought of by the author, the

commentator and the publisher as being subject to a single meaning, a correct understanding, an authorized reading. (CHARTIER, 2003, p. 123)

While the reader thinks about their own meanings during the act of reading, at the same time, the author and/or those involved in the preparation of a guide try to fit the reader into a framework that meets their objectives, for example by adopting ambiguous[7] positions.

> [...] all those involved in the world of writing are considered: authors, editors, booksellers, printers, critics, readers, spectators. Everyone takes part in the process of constructing meaning, understood from both a historical and sociological perspective (CHARTIER, 2003, p. 12).

The housewife could resort to reading gastronomic recipes while preparing the meal for the family or texts that question the idealization of women as perfect housewives, wives and mothers, by carrying the guide and/or magazine of the women's press through the spaces inside or outside the house.

In turn, those responsible for the creation, production, distribution/sale of behavioral manuals and magazines in the women's press also reflect on the uses they envision for their respective materials. *Tips and Practical Advice for the Home* has a paperback format. It could be inferred that one of the aims of this guide would be to accompany/advise women at all times in their lives, since it could be kept in cupboards/drawers or in handbags.

The practical guides designed essentially for the female public, containing themes related to the domestic environment and relationships with the family and with oneself, proved to be a source for the field of historical research, aiming to analyze the relationship between women and the home environment in the second half of the 20th century in Brazil. Reading it can help us understand what behaviors, values and education

[7]The adoption of ambiguous attitudes by the guides can be seen when, for example, the question of the husband's help with the household chores is raised.

were expected of females and males in Brazilian society at that time, where it is possible to see the coexistence of conflicts within the same space, linked to social demands and contexts (LUCA, 2012, p. 465).

Analyzing the guides helps, among other things, to problematize the motivations that led them to propagate certain advice - which was intended to be correct - to the female public.

According to Goncalves (2006, p. 110), "the use of this source [behavior manuals] [...] requires not taking the discourse as a norm, a mistake present in several works that have made use of this type of documentation." It is necessary to pay attention to aspects such as alternative behaviors, since between the indication of behaviors and their actual compliance, there are different positions in relation to what is proposed.

From this perspective, it is interesting to look at questions such as: how is the discourse intended by the guides being constructed? Who is it aimed at? How are the proposals based? What might be the intention behind propagating these values? In this way, it is interesting to look at the behavioral manuals *Biblioteca do Lar* and *Dicas e Conselhos Praticos para o Lar.*

A *Biblioteca do Lar - Grientagdo Indispensável a Familia* was written by Iside M. Bonini, under the supervision of Dr. Charles J. Fairbanks, and published by Grafica e Editora "Edigraf" S.A, in Sao Paulo (the year of publication is not disclosed - it is thought to be from the 1960s); it is the third volume in the series, which also includes the books *Boas Maneiras (em Familia)* and *Boas Maneiras (em Sociedade),* the latter from 1963. This guide covers topics such as home economics, motherhood, food care and appearance, basic first aid knowledge, among others; opting for formal language.

Figure 2 - Cover of the *Home Library* guide

[7]Source: Photo taken by the author

[7]Figure 3 - Thickness of the *Home Library* guide

Source: Photo taken by the author

Dicas e Conselhos Praticos para o Lar is made up of three

volumes, averaging 80 pages each, published by Renovada Livros Culturais Ltda (based in Rio de Janeiro). Reading all three volumes does not provide any information about the author or the year of publication. It is worth noting that *Dicas e Conselhos Praticos para o Lar,* like *Biblioteca do Lar, is* aimed at middle-class women.

The analysis of the discourse of the colleague0 *Dicas e Conselhos Praticos para o Lar* and *Biblioteca do Lar* allows us to assume that they date from the early 1960s, due to the fact that they are in line with the discourses constructed in Brazil in the early 1960s by the press, the state and medicine regarding industrialization, an ideal model of womanhood and domestic work.

Figure 4 - Cover of the guide *Practical Tips and Advice for the Home*

Source: Photo taken by the author

Figure 5 - Thickness of the guide *Practical Tips and Advice for the Home*

Source: Photo taken by the author

Tips and Practical Advice for the Home is written in informal language, seeking to get closer to the reader, making it sound like a "conversation between comadres", covering topics such as food, free time, the importance of being a housewife, relationships with the husband, hygiene and appearance, among others.

The behavioral manuals *Dicas e Conselhos Praticos para o Lar* and *Biblioteca do Lar* therefore aim to provide their target audience (women) with useful information for everyday life, covering domestic, family, matrimonial and maternal issues, with a view to solving the housewife's everyday problems.

Both guides also use images to communicate with readers. In the case of *Biblioteca do Lar, the* images are used to show the end result of a particular action proposed in the guide (tidying/cleaning the living room), how to carry out a particular procedure (patterns for making dresses or curtains), and in *Dicas e Conselhos Praticos para o Lar* (*Practical Tips and Advice for the Home*) only to illustrate the page (its first two volumes show an illustration of a woman in a small space before the title of each chapter).

> [...] numerous texts aim to cancel themselves out as discourse and produce in practice behaviors or conducts that are considered legitimate and useful. The arts of dying well, treatises on civility, books on practices are examples, among others, of these genres that aim to incorporate the necessary or convenient gestures into individuals (CHARTIER, 1988, p. 135).

Dicas e Conselhos Praticos para o Lar (Practical Tips and

Advice for the Home) and *Biblioteca do Lar (Home Library*) seek to show themselves to their readers as fundamental in helping to resolve issues - concerning domestic life and marital and family relationships - in women's daily lives. The guides' attempt to get closer to their readers may be indicative of the manuals' desire to propagate ways of behaving, acting and thinking for women, in which women's lives are confined to the domestic sphere and dedicated to caring for their husbands, children and home.

The intended reading of the two guides is for the reader to absorb the knowledge proposed by the author and/or those involved in their preparation. It should also be noted that the reading of behavioral manuals is faster and more practical, and is intended to instruct.

Instructing the housewife on *how, when* and *where* to use products from the consumer goods industry, such as household appliances, canned food, cleaning products, and the step-by-step running of household chores, is one of the trump cards used by the guides to justify their acquisition and permanence in the domestic environment.

4 What is the ideal housewife proposal?

As mentioned earlier, during the 1960s, a woman's happiness was still associated with the triad of marriage, motherhood and

household chores. The roles of men and women were clear and both were judged by how well they fulfilled them: the man had to provide for the household and the woman had to do the housework, take care of her husband and children, emotionally and physically.

Women were thought of as being confined to the home, since their participation in the labor market was seen as dangerous to the effective fulfillment of duties related to motherhood, marriage and domestic chores. The more domestic skills a woman had, the more she was valued by society at the time.

The idealization of women in The *Home Library* and *Practical Tips and Advice for the Home* converges on the same interpretation. The woman they wanted was ready to stand by her husband in all situations, even if their opinions differed; she took care of her good reputation and appearance; she showed good performance in carrying out household chores. It can thus be seen that, within the family model[8] , the woman occupied a special place as queen of the home, which reinforced the central role of the family in the woman's life and, it seems clear, her dependence on the marital lakes (BASSANEZI, 1996, p. 627).

The *Home Library* sees women as the "indispensable element for complete harmony in all the marvels created by the omnipotent hand of the Lord" (BIBLIOTECA DO LAR, s/d, p. 13). The woman-marriage-motherhood relationship is shown in an intrinsic way, in which a woman's

[8] According to BASSANEZI (1996), the dominant family model is the conjugal, nuclear one, with few children.

great victory is divided into two parts: getting a husband and being a mother.

> One day, in the life of every woman, there *will be* someone who *will feel* the same joy at being united with her chosen one; he won't repeat Adao's words verbatim, but the feelings and impulses will have their origin in that first encounter. This is the woman's first victory. Later on, her victory will be total, when it is completed by the great triumph of motherhood. (BIBLIOTECA DO LAR, s/d, p.13)

The housewife, according to the aforementioned guide, besides being associated with the triad of marriage, motherhood and domestic chores, had to dedicate her life to her home and family, even if she and her husband didn't have many resources to maintain them: "Your thought will be this: my home is no palace, but I will know how to transform it into a delightful corner where we can find peace and joy." (BIBLIOTECA DO LAR, s/d, p. 16).

In *Tips and Practical Advice for the Home,* after reading the three volumes, one can see the construction of a woman designed for the home environment, with added values that put her in charge of domestic and family activities. The aim is to build up a model of behavior in which the reader is patient, kind, condescending towards her husband's attitudes, even if he is rude; as well as encouraging him to carry out all the chores in the house, regardless of whether he likes it or not: the important thing is that he does it.

> The good example of courtesy and politeness should come from us. We should be very kind, generous, tolerant and considerate towards our husbands, certain that our children's attitude will always be a reflection of ours. (DICAS E CONSELHOS PRATICOS PARA O LAR, s/d, v. 1, p. 73)

In the second volume of the guide, four chapters (twenty-one in total) are devoted to highlighting the housewife. The aim is to create a positive image of the housewife, associating her not only with domestic work, but also with leisure and study. The importance of following the recommendations of Home Economics is emphasized.

> Housework is brutalizing when we neglect our spiritual life, which is why we need at least an hour a day for "us", whether it's getting up earlier or going to bed later, or after lunch, when the children go to school and Praxedes goes to the office... [...]
> [...] we will no longer be machines for looking after the house, the children and the maids... Even the work that seemed monotonous before will take on a different aspect when helped by an alert and positive spirit [and by Home Economics], which will show us how to work less and produce more. (TIPS AND PRACTICAL ADVICE FOR THE HOME, n.d., vol. 2, p. 30)

It's interesting to note that *Dicas e Conselhos Praticos para o Lar (Practical Tips and Advice for the Home) aims* to value the housewife. In this way, an attempt is made to build a relationship between women and the home environment, since, at various times, it is emphasized that it is important and gratifying for women to dedicate themselves diligently and painstakingly to household chores and caring for the family.

Kofes (2001) points out that the task of carrying out household chores is seen as feminine. Despite being an experience lived by some[9] women, the relationships established within it have various meanings, including the distinction between housewife and housewife.

According to the aforementioned author, the housewife is the woman who has the relationship of mother, wife and housewife with the family in the home; the one who hires the service of another woman - the housewife - to carry out the household chores. Both are seen as housewives, responsible for fulfilling/organizing household chores; however, the relationship established between them, despite the aforementioned "common ground", marks differences between them, due to the place they occupy in the household.

In this way, "the domestic (as a category) is therefore strategic. For, as well as referring to a place and how it functions, it refers both to family relationships and to relationships of a different order that take place

[9]Farias (1983) points out that it is possible to find women who experience different situations to the one presented as ideal: women as housewives, wives and mothers.

within it." (KOFES, 2001, p. 86).

In view of this observation about the devaluation of domestic work, Kofes (2001) and Farias (1983) raise the following question: is domestic work devalued because it is essentially a female activity? Or is domestic work devalued because it is carried out in the home? Or is domestic work devalued because it is domestic and female?

Indeed, it is worth noting Mello's (2011) observation about the valorization of domestic work:

> [...] giving visibility to domestic work [is] not simply because it is bad work and it is bad for the women who do it, but because it is important and necessary work for society, and it needs to be given more attention and recognized as work. (p. 70)

According to (2011), the issue of the invisibility of women's domestic work is one of the main points for thinking about the working conditions of housewives. The fact that tasks such as sweeping and cleaning the house, cooking, looking after the children and repairing clothes are not considered to be domestic work helps "to devalue these women [housewives] and [the emergence of] ideas such as the one that believes that housewives do nothing." (MELLO, 2011, p. 73). Bruschini (1990, p. 138) adds: "[some housewives emphasize that housework appears as] a service without any purpose or compensation, which only appears when it has not been done or has been done badly."

That's why it's important, as Mello (2011, p. 73) points out - quoting Danda Prado - to explain "that there is in fact an apprenticeship in domestic chores, and that performing domestic tasks requires specific knowledge."

When reading *Tips and Practical Advice for the Home,* one also notices a certain ambiguity in the proposal to set aside free time for women, since it is emphasized that this should take place after domestic chores and caring for the family have been completed, and it is mostly suggested that it should be spent within the confines of the home. The suggestions for activities to make the most of free time include cultivating friendships, going on excursions, making and receiving phone calls, writing and receiving letters, listening to good music, reading (happy and entertaining books), making culinary recipes; In other words, instead of proposing that women's time should be spent outside the home, the aim is to confine women more and more to the confines of the home, reinforcing the idea that household chores, caring for husbands and children, should come before leisure time.

The housewife envisioned by *Biblioteca do Lar* and *Dicas e Conselhos Praticos para o Lar (Home Library and Practical Tips and Advice for the Home*) should feel satisfaction in doing domestic work, full happiness with caring for the family; be elegant, healthy and beautiful (BASSANEZI, 1996).

5 What is the proposed division of work in the house?

According to Mello (2011), women are primarily responsible for carrying out domestic chores in the home. According to Bruschini (1990), domestic work is seen as an essential attribute of the female role. The possibility of being part of the labor market, or of hiring[10] the help of another woman to do the housework, does not exempt women from carrying out their daily activities, either by "compensating" for their time away from home by increasing their working hours with domestic chores, or by managing the household in order to ensure that it runs smoothly. And even if women were to dedicate themselves exclusively to caring for the home, their working hours would still be long.

With regard to household chores, Bassanezi (1996) points out that it wasn't common for husbands to help their wives - they were in charge of small repairs and/or tasks that required a lot of physical strength. If help did occur, it was not seen as an obligation, but as a "kindness"; citing a case analogous to what happened with financial help from the wife: it was not seen as obligatory and, most of the time, was not considered.

> Generally speaking, husbands believe that housework is really a woman's responsibility; therefore, when they share these duties with their partners, they always do so circumstantially, as help or cooperation. [...] The husband's help, when the need arises, is given with similar attitudes in any social segment and can be given, in this case, in any type of activity. (BRUSCHINI, 1990, p. 121)

Despite suggesting that the husband could collaborate in any type of domestic activity, if the need arose, Bruschini (1990) comments that, more often than not, this participation is more selective. The man carries out the domestic tasks that he feels most comfortable with, such as activities with the children, preparing meals and paying the bills.

[10] "[...] this other woman, the contractor, who generally has her own home, has two working days (both domestic)". (MELLO, 2011, p.60).

In addition to the question of need, according to Bruschini (1990), another factor that influences the husband's participation in domestic chores is his availability, measured, for example, by the amount of time he spends doing paid work in the labor market. Having the availability to carry out these tasks, however, does not necessarily mean that the man actually volunteers to do them.

Thus, as Mello (2011) points out, there is an unequal relationship

> [...] between the man and the woman in the home, where, even if they both arrive home from work at the same time, the domestic duties fall solely on the woman. These domestic duties include, in this case, in addition to looking after the house in general, serving the man who has come home "exhausted" from work. (p. 64)

In this sense, it is interesting to note a passage from the *Biblioteca do Lar*, which emphasizes that it is not obligatory for men to help with household chores. In the aforementioned guide, it is suggested that women ask their husbands for help with household chores:

> Obviously, [the housewife] shouldn't get her husband used to depending on her selflessness for everything; induce him to cooperate with you from the start. Household chores, at least some of them, don't make men inferior, as many people think. (BIBLIOTECA DO LAR, s/d, p. 22)

At the same time, however, as it expresses the option of dividing household chores between women and men, the *Home Library* does not exempt the female sex from total and non-transferable responsibility for looking after the home:

"But her [the housewife's] personal duties should not depend on her husband's incessant help. It is her undeniable duty to carry them out if she is not ill or unable to do so" (BIBLIOTECA DO LAR, s/d, p. 23).

Despite suggesting (explicitly or not) that the man should take part in household chores, "sparing" the woman from some household chores, *the Biblioteca do Lar* emphasizes that she could not count on her husband's help to fulfill her role as a housewife. It can therefore be inferred that it was up to the man to decide whether or not to help his wife with the day-to-day running of the household. If he did, there were specific tasks for the man (the guides don't specify which ones); if not, the woman had to conform and do all the chores herself, without complaining or insisting on receiving help.

Tips and Practical Advice for the Home, on the other hand, adopts a slightly different attitude to the *Home Library.* Instead of suggesting that the husband help with the household chores, in the chapter entitled "Participation of the Family" (first volume), the plot of which is about the division of household chores, he expresses that it is the children who should take on this role: "It is not possible (nor very good politics) to transform the husbands, but it is in our hands to better guide the children." (TIPS AND PRACTICAL ADVICE FOR THE HOME, n.d., vol. 1, p. 63).

Bruschini (1990) points out that the fact that children are in the home can have different meanings for housewives. At the same time as it can represent extra domestic work for women, as they have to devote attention to their children in terms of physical and emotional care - and influence whether or not they enter the job market - it can also denote a certain flexibility for the housewife to carry out other tasks that are not necessarily related to the domestic sphere:

> [...] the presence of children of a certain age in the family can mean [...] the possibility of a woman seeking better work opportunities outside the home, leaving an older daughter, for example, with responsibility for the home and even for her younger siblings. (BRUSCHINI, 1990, p. 82)

Reading the three volumes of *Dicas e Conselhos Praticos para o Lar (Practical Tips and Advice for the Home)* does not show, however, that the housewife's intention in having her children help her with the household chores was so that she could look for opportunities for a paid job in the labor market, since women's participation in the aforementioned environment is not considered by the Collection - despite the fact that, in some passages, the three volumes point to examples of American women who both work outside the home and do household chores. It is clear, therefore, that despite showing the example of the USA, Brazilian women were not encouraged to do the same.

This guide points out that although women want their husbands to help them with the daily chores, they "have a long-standing and ingrained 'lack of practice', inherited from the Cave Man" (TIPS AND PRACTICAL ADVICE FOR THE HOME, n.d., vol. 1, p. 9), in order to do this; however, the male sex is invited to take part in the preparation of gastronomic recipes. According to *Dicas e Conselhos Praticos para o Lar (Practical Tips and Advice for the Home)*, the kitchen is associated with women; however, men should be encouraged to participate and "experiment at will" (DICAS E CONSELHOS PRATICOS PARA O LAR, s/d, v. 1, p. 9) with the art of cooking. Although it is women who spend more time in the kitchen, it is men who receive the biggest and best titles and praise for their good performance in preparing gastronomic recipes. It can therefore be inferred that working in the kitchen is obligatory for women, while for men it is sporadic and worthy of the highest honors.

6 Home Economics

In addition to her responsibilities related to household chores, the ideal housewife should also study in order to improve her performance in the activities to be carried out in the home. However, according to Bassanezi (1996), in the second half of the 20th century there was an increase in the level of schooling for women, but the study aimed at by the two behavioral manuals is mainly restricted to one area - Home Economics - which highlights, according to the author, that schooling for women is valued when it is associated with the benefits it brings in terms of fulfilling the duties of mother, wife and housewife.

The study of home economics was stimulated, for example, by guides aimed primarily at women (addressing the care they should take of their home, family and marriage) in the 1960s, since

> [...] the housewife must be both the consumer and the administrator of the home. She is therefore left with the responsibility of controlling consumption, which becomes an activity to be organized and planned rigorously, including installment purchases and long-term projects. (PASSERINI, 1991, p. 387)

However, it's worth pointing out that not all women who studied Home Economics were necessarily dedicated to carrying out this activity (in rural or urban areas) in a professional capacity. There were women who applied the lessons they learned in the domestic sphere.

It is interesting to understand, therefore, that in the 1950s and 1960s, "[...] the vision of Home Economics was identified with the 'functionality of the home' and family relationships were marked by the performance of differentiated, asymmetrical and complementary roles by family members." (AMARAL, 2000, p. 10).

Brazil's economic development brought new opportunities for schooling. In the case of women, the opportunities were related to an increase in the level of schooling and participation in the labor market. However, this did not mean that equal education for men and women was being advocated, nor did it mean an end to gender discrimination in this respect. The growing demand for manpower in the bureaucratic, financial and educational services, in both the public and private sectors, helped to encourage education at secondary and higher levels.

> However, despite the social obstacles to female education (which grow as the level of schooling increases), it contributes to significant changes in the family and social *status of* women and, ultimately, to important questions and transformations in male-female relations (BASSANEZI, 1996, p.225).

As women gained access to knowledge that had previously been seen as the privilege of men, the idea began to spread that studying for women could contribute to their "moral condition". However, the idea that the female sex should continue to occupy its - primordial, essential - place as housewife, wife and mother was emphasized. A highly educated woman could pose a danger to marriage, male power and the established family model. Thus, despite the new educational possibilities for women, they had to continue to follow the ideal woman's role model, be the perfect wife, be responsible for the harmony of the home.

In Brazil, the first Home Economics degree course was created in the 1950s, in Vigosa-MG; its target audience was preferably female; and its foundations followed, according to Amaral Junior (2013, p. 278), the "molds of an American nuclear family structure and preaching the *status quo* of a 'feminine place' in the family and in society". Throughout the 1960s and 1970s,[11] other higher education courses in Home Economics

---

[11]It should be noted, however, that "The circumstances that led to the creation of higher education courses and even courses in Home Economics at secondary level and in agro-technical schools reveal the interest of the governments of the time, in the 1950s and 1960s, in developing policies for rural development and female education for the structuring and functionality of the family." (AMARAL, 2000, p. 32). To find out more about the objectives behind the creation of Higher Degrees in Home Economics in Brazil, readAMARAL, Celia Chaves Gurgel do. **Fundamentos da Economia Domestica:** perspectiva da condigao feminina e das relações de genero. Fortaleza: EUFC, 2000.

were created in Brazil, such as Rio de Janeiro in 1963, Sao Paulo in 1967 and Ceara in 1972. These courses belonged to both state and federal public universities and private institutions. The subjects of the Higher Course in Home Economics included nutrition, clothing, education, childcare, education, art and recreation.

In the 1960s, the study of Home Economics, according to Amaral (2000, p. 15), was predominantly female, and focused on issues such as rationalizing time and space in the home, the best way to use family resources, and how to (re)use food.

The male and female spheres were separated. The domestic economist was prepared to assist families in carrying out activities that were considered feminine, carried out within the domestic sphere. According to Amaral (2000), since the practice of managing and organizing household chores was associated with the female sex, this helps us understand why an intrinsic relationship was established between women and Home Economics, in which the study was mostly carried out by women. "This fact was enough to explain all the sexually differentiated treatment in the institutions where women professionals have worked, and in the school system." (AMARAL, 2000, p. 10).

The *Home Library* emphasizes that *""Home Economics,* in its true sense, means intelligent management of one's own assets, with the aim of obtaining the maximum result from them with the minimum expenditure or loss" (BIBLIOTECA DO LAR, s/d, p. 35). Furthermore, this study and

> [...] the main responsibility for the balance of the home and for the social peace of a people. [Domestic] education in this respect is necessary, because the collaboration of each person, whether large or small, in this direction makes it possible to correct, if not mitigate, economic crises and other social problems. (BIBLIOTECA DO LAR, s/d, p. 35)

The *Home Library* also warns that,

> If [the housewife] doesn't have a minimum of basic knowledge about home economics, which depends to a certain extent on a reasonable culture or a well-oriented conscience, it becomes very difficult to organize the home perfectly. (BIBLIOTECA DO LAR, s/d, p. 36)

This means that women had to make an effort to gain access to the basic principles of home economics, in order to perform their role as housewife, mother and wife well, and also to contribute to the preservation of the ideal family model desired by Brazilian society in the 1960s.

One of the tips on home economics expressed by the guides can be seen in the *Home Library,* concerning the preparation of meals:

> When preparing lunch, also provide dinner. Make enough rice and beans, or broth, for both meals. Leave vegetables cooked or cleaned, depending only on last-minute seasoning. By following this system, you'll save time and, at the same time, you'll save a lot of fuel. (BIBLIOTECA DO LAR, s/d, p. 26)

If the housewife chose to follow the proposed teaching, she would gain the following advantages: time savings, practicality, "comfort" (she wouldn't have to cook dinner in the evening and could devote herself to other domestic activities), she would learn how to use food, she would help her husband (she wouldn't waste fuel on the stove).

Dicas e Conselhos Praticos para o Lar (Practical Tips and Advice for the Home) sets out a different position from the *Home Library on* the study intended for women. According to the Colleague, education for women is contradictory, as it offers women the chance to study on the condition that they already have children, so that they can combine caring for the home and studying.

In the chapter entitled "Age and studies" in the second volume, women are encouraged to continue their studies - interrupted by marriage and the arrival of children. It is indicated, however, that this should take place in areas such as teaching, music, the arts, gastronomy and social work.

"Study, when you are old enough, is very beneficial, because you will enter it with all your experience and maturity and the strength of a true vocation, slowly developed" (DICAS E CONSELHOS PRATICOS PARA O LAR, s/d, vol. 2, p. 42). It follows, then, that prolonged domestic experience would be a positive aspect for women, as it would allow them to develop the knowledge they have learned in practice, and make them reflect on their professional vocation.

However, the question must be asked: what if women don't want to stop studying? If they already choose to follow their professional vocation? If they wanted to choose to continue their studies in areas considered masculine?

During the reading, it is possible to see the use of mathematical, chemical and historical concepts, both for the preparation of gastronomic recipes and to emphasize the "power" that spices[12] can give to meals, as well as for the best use of food measurements, the use of the gas stove, among other aspects.

> It's not difficult to prepare a good barbecue. If you don't have your own barbecue, you can cook it on your gas stove. There's no danger of poisoning, as many people think, preferring charcoal. Because the carbon monoxide found in stove gas is the result of the imperfect combustion of coal, and gas is a derivative of coal. So the monoxide (poisonous gas) exists in the extinguished gas and not in the flame, because when it burns the monoxide is transformed into dioxide, which is an inert gas that exists in the atmosphere. (TIPS AND PRACTICAL ADVICE FOR THE HOME, s/d, vol. 1, p.19)

It is clear that the authors of this book are interested in showing women how important it is to have a healthy mental life, since they need to express themselves as pleasant companions for men. This healthy mental life, however, is limited to recreational and joyful reading, writing letters to family and friends, and family life, because true happiness lies in the

[12]"They aroused ambition and lust in men, as if they were gold! They served as a stimulus for great adventures, as we learn in our own history: the Portuguese admiral Pedro Alvares Cabral, "when he went to India in search of spices..." (Dicas e Conselhos Praticos para o Lar, s/d, vol. 2, p. 34-35).

confines of the home, with the husband and children.

> However, there are creatures like Totoca, who decided to study just now, when she has three little children! She is the daughter of an industrialist, and her husband holds a high position, earning around 900,000 cruzeiros a month! And this little mother has just discovered that she has a vocation for architecture - only now, because when she was studying she didn't care about books, but about playing hooky to the movies or meeting her boyfriend. Now she says: "An architect can earn a lot of money! It's very nice to be an architect! I'll only be happy the day I become an architect!" (TIPS AND PRACTICAL ADVICE FOR THE HOME, n.d., vol. 1, p. 83-85).

In the environment idealized by the book, the character Totoca represents the example of a housewife, a family mother, who should not be followed. This trait can be seen when - in the chapter entitled "Desiring the Impossible", from the first volume - the authors point out that the character's desire to study architecture is unnecessary, since her husband earns a salary, it is inferred, sufficient to support the household, and her father worked as an industrialist; as well as suggesting that the time spent studying - which she wasted - should have been put to good use before married life and the arrival of children.

Although the study of architecture was seen as an "impossible desire", the study of home economics was encouraged at the same time, with a view to women becoming better prepared to manage the home, learning how to organize their time better, solve household problems, educate their children, improve their cultural and spiritual level, and plan household financial expenses. "It is necessary to look for ways to keep women at home and divert them away from wage-earning" (PERROT, 2005, p. 256).

In the third volume of *Practical Tips and Advice for the Home,* the chapter entitled "Introduction to Home Accounting" explains this segment, emphasizing the importance of organizing the household. At the same time, it explains how income and expenditure are forecast, how records are kept; it points out that it is interesting to pay attention to the fact that the advertising for a particular product may not match the reality, that it is important to compare nails; it explains the difference between short-, medium- and long-term purchases, and what the advantages and disadvantages are of buying from supermarkets, corner stores and street markets.

> The housewives of the future will need to study home economics from the good old days of "mama's house", so that when their turn comes, they will be perfectly capable of solving, in the best possible way, all those complex and unnerving problems that make up the "art" of being a real housewife. (TIPS AND PRACTICAL ADVICE FOR THE HOME, n.d., v. 1, p. 37)

One can see the commitment made in the pages of this book to conveying to women the importance of an education geared towards the domestic environment and good relations with their husbands and children. "Both study and professions must enable a woman to carry out her professional (minor) and domestic (primordial) tasks well." (PERROT, 2005, p. 251).

These characteristics of Home Economics are noticeable both in guides and in magazines in the women's press, when they cover the "step by step" of domestic activities to be carried out more "efficiently". The concern with the insertion of women into molds that were in line with the desire to relate women more and more to the confines of the home is perceived, albeit indirectly, *in O Livro do Lar (The Home Book)* when it informs us which foods contain a large amount of calories, carbohydrates, proteins, mineral salts and vitamins; in addition to highlighting the importance of making a menu of the week's meals, in order to better organize and distribute the time spent on each task and avoid unnecessary trips to the market to buy food that might be missing.

They are taught how to make a menu: the housewife should pay attention to the tastes of each member of the family, the season, and try to make the family's diet well-balanced, including proteins, calories, carbohydrates, vitamins and minerals. It was also essential for the housewife to try to be creative when preparing recipes and to offer a variety of dishes.

It should be noted, however, that these characteristics of Home Economics - associated with the female sex and found in guides and magazines in the women's press - cannot be understood as belonging to the female sex. As Amaral (2000, p. 12) points out, it is worth emphasizing that "the teachings of the home universe, the knowledge concerning improving the quality of family life are not naturally incorporated into women.".

Despite the fact that, especially in the 1960s and early 1970s, Home Economics did not express (AMARAL, 2000, p. 38) much concern about carrying out more in-depth studies on "Family, Women, Gender, Consumption and Sustainable Development", it is interesting to think about the need to question the bases that have led Home Economics to be associated, preferentially, with the female sex; and to problematize the link built between women and domestic activities.

7 The use of "modernity" in the domestic sphere: saving time and hygiene

According to *Biblioteca do Lar* and *Dicas e Conselhos Praticos para o Lar,* "modernity" in the domestic sphere refers to the use of products from the consumer goods industry in the home, such as household appliances, canned food and cleaning products, so that housewives can carry out household chores quickly and practically.

Practical Tips and Advice for the Home makes this objective explicit when, in its first volume, in the chapter entitled "Modern Woman", it states that: "We [housewives] must be progressive, experimenting with the extraordinary machines of today, which are designed to make our tasks easier, doing for us a difficult part of the daily routine." (TIPS AND PRACTICAL ADVICE FOR THE HOME, n.d., v. 1, p. 55)

Silva Filho (2008) points out that, due to the close connection between household appliances and the daily lives of men and women,

> Refrigerators, fans, washing machines, vacuum cleaners, irons, mixers, lamps... [...] they are not just purely instrumental, but become extensions of the body, increasing its abilities, training its gestures, making the most of its efforts. In fact, through them it is possible to detect changes in ordinary life, vibrations in that tenuous and sensitive cord that connects the existences of individuals in society. (p. 5)

The relationship between women and products from the consumer goods industry cannot be understood solely as an immediate exchange, aimed at performing some circumstantial domestic service. As Silva Filho (2008, p. 6) points out, "[...] these electrical appliances cannot be understood as if they were unrelated to the material and cultural space in which they are inserted".

In this way, it is worth questioning the proposal that the guides make to women to organize and distribute their time throughout the day in a rational way, as well as the simultaneous presentation of the step-by-step process for carrying out household chores, in order to save time and (re)use the resources available in the home environment.

"[...] the incorporation of household appliances and other accessories (bathrooms with surfaces, functional kitchens, smooth and shiny floors, lined ceilings, light and ergonomic furniture) [...]" (SILVA FILHO, 2008, p. 9) could mean "comfort", practicality and time-saving for women's domestic daily lives.

Mello (2011), when discussing domestic work for women, comments on the understanding of two researchers, Maria Angeles Duran and Cristina Torres, on the relationship between technology and domestic work. The first researcher, despite observing that technology has helped to reduce the physical effort made by women when carrying out household chores, points out that women's working hours in the home remain long. The other researcher points out that the use of electrical appliances in the domestic sphere helps to reduce the time women devote to household chores, as well as having implications for the quality and quantity of daily tasks.

Bruschini (1990) comments that

> Several studies have shown that technology applied to the domestic space has done little to change the overall amount of time consumed in carrying out household chores [...] However, the possession of certain household appliances can provide families with some facilities in carrying out domestic chores and even guide different arrangements in everyday life. (p. 134)

Biblioteca do Lar (Home Library) and *Dicas e Conselhos Praticos para o Lar (Practical Tips and Advice for the Home*) understand the insertion of products from the consumer goods industry as a beneficial factor for women's daily lives, as they could reduce the time spent doing household chores and use it for other activities. It is worth asking, however:

would the woman use her free time in her own way or by doing other activities that would satisfy the other members of the family? Could the housewife really rest and do something that really interested her?

> In the evening, after dinner and when you've finished your household chores, it's a good idea to listen to a radio program (or television if there is one); it's a useful distraction [...] The news is particularly interesting, because it tells you what's going on in the world and provides a momentary escape from personal problems. However, it is advisable to occupy your hands while listening to the radio with some kind of work: embroidery, knitting, metal darning, etc.; the work is very profitable without you realizing it. The radio also announces the time of your well-deserved rest. (BIBLIOTECA DO LAR, s/d, p. 34)

Saving time is one of the main issues raised by the *Home Library* and *Practical Tips and Advice for the Home.* This topic is presented as fundamental to the proper performance of the domestic tasks assigned to the housewife, as well as to the proper functioning of all the activities that take place in the home, whether domestic or not (if the woman manages to save time, she will be "freer" to "look after herself" and her family).

The *Home Library* emphasizes that,

> First and foremost, however, it is vitally important to know how to save time. Darwin put forward the concept that "we can only accomplish our purposes by saving the minutes". So let's give practical application to every minute of the day, never forgetting that order, organized work, set schedules and the habit of respecting them are essential factors for progress. (BIBLIOTECA DO LAR, s/d, p. 55)

In *Practical Tips and Advice for the Home,* time-saving appears to also regulate the housewife's level of efficiency:
"We housewives can't waste any time! We receive daily
24 hours exactly, not a minute more or less. The use we make of these precious hours determines our degree of efficiency." (s/d, v. 1, p.
21).

The way in which the two behavioral manuals understand time saving is in line with Taylorism's understanding of the same subject, which, according to Rago (2003, p. 14), was disseminated and applied in the second quarter of the 20th century in the world's industries, determining the organization of contemporary work.

> As a method of rationalizing production and thus making it possible to increase work productivity by "saving time", eliminating unnecessary gestures and superfluous behaviour within the production process, the Taylor system perfected the social division of labour introduced by the factory system, definitively ensuring the control of workers' time by the ruling class. (RAGO, 2003, p. 10)

However, it is not the purpose of this research to go into the details of the Taylorism method or the consequences of its adoption, or not, by the most diverse sectors of society in the 20th century. The aim of this research is to understand the relationship between the time-saving proposed by the Taylorist method and the time-saving proposed by the guides for housewives.

This proposition of connection is commented on in RAGO (2003), when it is pointed out that the influence of Taylorism went beyond the walls of the factories:

> [...] this method of intensifying production in a shorter space of time ended up penetrating and determining even activities that take place outside the walls of the factory. Perhaps this is its main success. After all, in many areas of society, in sport or in domestic work, people try to get the most out of their time, not infrequently obeying the rules and instructions dictated by "scientific" guidelines and guides for rationalizing how we act, feel and think. Newsstands, as well as television programs, are now full of these manuals and recipes that claim to teach you how to make the most of your time, how to make the most of your day, how to do a lot more exercise in the same amount of time, etc. (P. 11)

Solutions for increasing productivity while avoiding wasting time are seen in *Practical Tips and Advice for the Home*, which states: "Time, when used correctly, becomes one of our best allies and is of great importance in our lives. We need to learn to think in terms of hours, for work, play and rest" (vol. 1, p. 21).

In the chapter entitled "Time passes" in the first volume of this guide, we hear about the importance of valuing time and not wasting it.

> We need to be aware of the time that passes and make good use of it, putting it to good use and not letting ourselves be ruled by it, which leads us to live in constant hurry and fright: - Suddenly we look at the clock and see 2.30, remember the appointment for 3, and rush off to be late! (p. 22)

Aiming to highlight the good return the housewife would receive from organizing her time during the day, he continues:

> You'll be able to enjoy quiet hours of recreation with the time you have free. It will be like a valuable gift to yourself. But whatever you do with it, don't waste it on people or things that don't mean anything to you: - learn to rest your heart with double satisfaction:
> There are some very unpleasant jobs to be done around the house. Schedule time for these tasks, do them on time and enjoy a well-deserved rest with a clear conscience. For example, do you know how long it takes to bake a cake? Try marking it on your watch the next time you bake. Our Crazy Cake is very quick: it takes exactly 13 minutes to make, bake and wash the bowl. This way, when you're short of time, you'll know exactly which recipe to choose so that you don't get off track: - you'll know if there's enough time to complete the job. (TIPS AND PRACTICAL ADVICE FOR THE HOME, n.d., vol. 1, p. 22-23)

The housewife's reward would be to have more time to carry out extra activities that would essentially benefit the other members of the family. Contradictorily, despite ensuring that the housewife should not let herself be ruled by time, *Practical Tips and Advice for the Home* stresses that all the activities she carries out should be organized and programmed, always taking into account the time spent.

According to Rago (2003, p. 100-101): "In practice, it is impossible to demand that a worker perform 'the one good method' all the time and at the same pace imposed by management. After all, the very functioning of the norms and rhythms imposed depend on the worker's acceptance [...]."

It's important to consider that, although there are suggestions of ways of doing things, ways of leading, ways of managing household chores, the housewife is not obliged to accept everything willingly. It's worth noting the possible existence of conflicts in the domestic sphere as a result of the burdens placed on women.

In the case of another female to help with the housework, this is mentioned, not mostly, by the *Biblioteca do Lar.* This behavioral manual mentions the possibility of having a maid, but does not exempt the housewife from the responsibility of "watching over" the work done, managing the material resources of the house and the domestic order. *Hints and Practical Advice for the Home* assumes that it is a disadvantage to have a maid: it is the housewife herself who must "modernize" and take care of the house on her own.

According to the *Home Library,*

> To these [women who work outside the home] we are obliged to say: your home needs you, it demands your affection, your care, if you make a point of providing your loved ones with the comfort they crave. So, a little more sacrifice, because women have received the greatest share of this since time immemorial. She is not allowed to avoid this inheritance, unless she prefers to ruin the family happiness that depends on it. Remember: marriage has given you the lion's share of responsibility and in order to cope with it, you have to multiply yourself every hour of the day, thinking first and foremost of the good you can do for your family, thanks precisely to your sacrifices. (p.21).

This is how *Dicas e Conselhos Praticos para o Lar,* in the second volume, in the chapter entitled "O problema das empregadas", states that it is difficult for the Brazilian housewife to get "good maids for reasonable wages" (p. 49). Therefore,

> The only way to solve the problem [of having another woman help with household chores], economically and satisfactorily, is to get to grips with our kitchen, modernize the facilities and our way of eating, using different, tasty and easy-to-make recipes that will give us pleasure and joy in doing them. (TIPS AND PRACTICAL ADVICE FOR THE HOME, n.d., vol. 2, p. 50-51).

Kofes (2001, p. 34-35) teaches that the term "domestic" can be defined as feminine and as defining femininity, which could indicate a common recognition among women, due to the production of the domestic as feminine. This word, however, can also express the distinction between female subjects, i.e. those who are in charge of carrying out female tasks and those who occupy female positions in family relationships.

In addition to saving time, hygiene is also highly valued by both guides. A clean, tidy and organized house is an indication that the housewife is making an effort to keep her home in harmony. The importance of hygiene is made clear in a comment from the *Home Library*.

> In the first place, general and meticulous cleanliness is the basis of well-being and dignity; where dirt prevails, charm disappears. The good housewife should know the basic principles of true home hygiene and practice will help her to maintain the most scrupulous hygiene. (p. 16)

Silva (2007, p. 202) points out that hygiene is a factor that, in addition to having been decisive for the transformations that took place in the kitchen space in Brazilian urban centers between 1870 and 1930 - due to the spread of epidemics and the need to clean and organize cities - also aroused the interest of "suppliers of urban services and objects for consumption [...], especially domestic ones".

The *Home Library* illustrates this aspect by highlighting the use of a specific cleaning product to clean the bathroom: "[...] the bathroom is cleaned [...] flush and pour in a good disinfectant, and [the housewife] can choose 'Lysoforme Bruto' which is one of the best." (p. 25). In addition to suggesting how to clean the bathroom step by step, the guide also indicates which cleaning product is the most suitable to use. There is thus a relationship between the guide and the advertiser of products from the consumer goods industry, which is essentially aimed at housewives.

The space in the house, the furniture, the utensils, the materials and the food used to prepare meals all deserved special attention from the housewife. *Tips and Practical Advice for the Home,* when addressing what the ideal housewife should be like, emphasizes that, in relation to the domestic sphere, the woman should pay attention to all aspects of food, from its nutritional value to the way it is prepared and the means used to fulfill the recipes. There are also suggestions for practices to be adopted when handling food (it is better to hold the food in your hand and wash it under running water to remove impurities, rather than sticking it on a fork and washing it quickly) as well as household appliances.

"And so our lives evolve every day. As we ourselves become more aware of the importance of good nutrition and modern equipment, we become more interested in cooking." (v. 2, p. 14).

According to Silva (2007, p. 204), organizing and cleaning the household space is also related to the arrangement of household furniture, in order to achieve better efficiency in carrying out household chores. The arrangement of furniture and the attention paid to its upkeep are examples of the care that housewives should take when tidying up their living spaces, as neglecting these aspects can interfere with the proper development of their home care duties, and hinder the efficiency of their work.

The housewife, following the line of thought adopted by *Biblioteca do Lar* and *Dicas e Conselhos Praticos para o Lar,* had to be efficient in everyday domestic life, save time while doing household chores, and value hygiene; in order to fit the profile of "modern woman", "efficient housewife", and insert the notion of "modernity" into the domestic sphere.

Conclusion

During the second half of the 20th century, Brazil witnessed the struggle of women to gain rights, not only social and political rights - which were also seen at the end of the 19th century - but also rights concerning sexuality, the body, violence against women and labor issues. "As examples [of this struggle] we can cite: the right to 'have children when you want, if you want', the fight against domestic violence, the demand that household chores should be divided [...]" (PEDRO, 2005, p. 80). The universal status that men had acquired was questioned.

> [...] the big question that all [the participants in the feminist movements] wanted to answer [...] was why women, in different societies, were subjected to male authority, in the most diverse forms and to the most diverse degrees. Thus, they realized, it didn't matter what the culture defined as women's activity: this activity was always disqualified in relation to what men, from the same culture, did. (PEDRO, 2005, p. 83)

Mello (2011) points out that, despite being a responsibility perceived as feminine, in her studies she found no information before 1970 about the problematization of domestic work by feminist movements. After this period, the factors that helped to raise questions about the issue are related, among other things, to the cloistered aspect with which domestic work came to be symbolized, and the cultural upheavals of the time.

> Perhaps the greatest achievement of the young feminists of the 1970s and 1980s - often unknown to the younger generations - is the recognition that there are *other ways of being a woman,* beyond the idealized roles of wife, mother and housewife. (PEDRO, 2012, p. 256)

Throughout this research, we can see the intention of the sources used to convey to women the importance of being a mother, wife and housewife. At the same time, we realize that this purpose did not happen in a continuous, linear way. *Livro do Lar, Biblioteca do Lar and Dicas e Conselhos Praticos para o Lar* had to adopt strategies in order to bring readers closer to their ideas, while emphasizing the "modern" character with which they were being associated.

It can be seen that the sources used, at the same time as giving tips on how to make the home a harmonious and pleasant environment (for whom? For the wife? For the husband?), sought to make the reader become a more practical and efficient housewife, by spreading the notions of usefulness, time-saving and domestic economy, since they needed to manage the domestic sphere better and dedicate time "just for themselves".

We should therefore ask ourselves: is the writing of *The Home Book, The Home Library and Practical Tips and Advice for the Home* a way of opposing the discourse adopted by the feminist movements, especially those that took place in the 1960s and 1970s? Why was there a need to remind women of the importance of being a housewife?

Reading the sources analyzed, one can infer that the discourses were eager to shape the dissemination of a lifestyle for the modern housewife. The desired model of woman could adopt certain modernizing attitudes in her daily domestic life, such as the division of time throughout the day to carry out household chores, the application of the teachings of Home Economics to better manage the home, the acquisition/use of products from the consumer goods industry (such as household appliances, canned food, cleaning products) and household utensils to "make it easier" to carry out household activities.

However, despite the modern character that was intended to be given to those who adopted these attitudes - the housewife should be "efficient and practical" - the "modern woman" could only be modern within the domestic sphere.

The tips and practical advice on "modernity" confined the female sex to the confines of the home and sought to disseminate mechanisms that would help housewives to carry out their domestic duties and care for the family quickly, practically and efficiently. It was not intended to disseminate a behavior in which women questioned their rights regarding sexuality, the body, violence against women, work issues, in the private and public sphere.

It is therefore interesting to try to problematize the arrangement of structures that form the basis of stereotypes which refer to women as ideal models of mothers, wives and housewives, plus qualities such as tolerance, kindness and condescension, and associated with the domestic sphere and selected public spheres (a career in teaching early childhood education was seen as an extension of a woman's maternal "nature") - while emphasizing the heterogeneous nature of the female sex, expressing significant distinctions both in relation to the male sex and to each other.

Sources

HOUSEHOLD MANUALS

Iside M. **Indispensable Guidance for the Family**. Home Library Collection. Sao Paulo: Grafica e Editora "EDIGRAF" S.A, N/C.

TIPS AND PRACTICAL ADVICE FOR THE HOME. Rio de Janeiro: Renovada Livros Culturais Ltda. v. 1.

Rio de Janeiro: Renovada Livros Culturais Ltda. v. 2.

Rio de Janeiro: Renovada Livros Culturais Ltda. v. 3.

MAGAZINES

THE HOME BOOK. Sao Paulo: Editora Abril Ltda., 1964.

References

AMARAL, Celia Chaves Gurgel do. **Fundamentals of Home Economics: a** perspective on the female condition and gender relations. Fortaleza: EUFC, 2000.

AMARAL JUNIOR, Jose Carlos do. Education for women: a historical analysis of the teaching of Home Economics in Brazil. **Revista HISTEDBR On-line**, Campinas, n. 52, p. 275-285, Sep. 2013.

BASSANEZI, Carla (coord. de textos); PRIORE, Mary Del (org.). **Historia das mulheres no Brasil**. 2. ed. Sao Paulo: Contexto, 1997.

BASSANEZI, Carla Beozzo. **Turning the pages, revisiting** women: women's magazines and male-female relations, 1945-1964. Rio de Janeiro: Civilizagao Brasileira, 1996.

BRUSCHINI, Maria Cristina Aranha. **Woman, home and family**: daily life in the middle classes of São Paulo. Sao Paulo: Fundagao Carlos Chagas: Vertice, Editora Revista dos Tribunais, 1990.

BUITONI, Dulcilia Schroeder. **Women's press.** 2.ed. Sao Paulo: Atica, 1990.

. **Mulher de papel:** the representation of women in the Brazilian press. Sao

Paulo: Loyola, 1981.

CHARTIER, Roger. **Cultural History**: between practices and representations. Translated by Maria Manuela Galhardo. 2ª ed. Rio de Janeiro: Bertrand Brasil; Lisbon: Difel. 2002.

. **Forms and meaning**. Written culture: between distinction and appropriation. Translated by Maria de Lourdes Meirelles Matencio. Campinas, SP: Mercado das Letras; Associagao de Leitura do Brasil (ALB), 2003.

DUARTE, Ana Rita Fonteles. **Carmen da Silva**: feminism in the Brazilian press. Fortaleza: Expressao Grafica e Editora, 2005.

FARIAS, Zaira Ary. **Domesticity:** female 'captivity'? Rio de Janeiro: Achiame, 1983.

FIGUEIRA, Servulo A. The "modern" and the "archaic" in the new Brazilian family: notes on the invisible dimension of social change. *In:* FIGUEIRA, Servulo A. **A new family?** The modern and the archaic in the Brazilian middle-class family. Rio de Janeiro: Jorge Zahar Editor, 1987.

GONCALVES, Eliane; PINTO, Joana Plaza. Reflections and problems of intergenerational "transmission" in Brazilian feminism. **Cad. Pagu**, Campinas, n. 36, p. 25-46, June 2011. Available at: <http://www.scielo.br/scielo.php?script=sci_arttext&pid=S0104-83332011000100003&lng=en&nrm=iso>. Accessed on: May 8, 2015.

HIGONNET, Anne. Women, images and representations. *In:* DUBY, Georges; PERROT, Michelle. **History of Women in the West**. Porto: Afrontamento, 1991. 5v.

KOFES, Suely. **Mulher, mulheres** - identity, difference and inequality in the relationship between employers and domestic workers. Campinas, SP: Editora da Unicamp, 2001.

LIPOVETSKY, Gilles. **The third woman. Permanence and revolution of the feminine**. Translated by Maria Joao Batalha Reis. Piaget Institute, 1997.

LUCA, Tania Regina de. Mulher em revista. *In:* BASSANEZI, Carla (org.); PEDRO, Joana Maria. **New History of Women in Brazil**. Sao Paulo: Contexto, 2012.

MELLO, Soraia Carolina de. **An invisible profession: Housewife (1970-**

1989). Perseu: Historia, Memoria e Politica, v. 7, p. 59-83, 2011.
MIRA, Maria Celeste. **The reader and the newsstand:** the segmentation of culture in the 20th century. Sao Paulo: Olho d'Agua/Fapesp, 2001.

MORIN, Edgar. **Mass culture in the 20th century**. With the collaboration of Irene Nahoum. Translation by Agenor Soares Santos. 3 ed. Rio de Janeiro: Forense Universitaria, 2003.

. **Mass culture in the 20th century:** neurosis. Translated by Maura Ribeiro Sardinha. 9 ed. Rio de Janeiro: Forense Universitaria, 2005.

PADRO, Luiz Carlos Delorme; EARP, Fabio Sa. The Brazilian "miracle": accelerated growth, international integration and income concentration (1967-1973). *In:* FERREIRA, Jorge; DELGADO, Lucilia de Almeida Neves. **Republican Brazil.** Rio de Janeiro: Civilizagao Brasileira, 2003. 4v.

PASSERINI, Luisa. Women, consumption and mass culture. *In:* DUBY, Georges; PERROT, Michelle. **History of Women in the West**. Porto: Afrontamento, 1991. 5v.

PERROT, Michelle. **Women or the silences of history**. Translated by Viviane Ribeiro. Bauru, SP: EDUSC, 2005.

PINSKY, Carla Bassanezi. The era of rigid models. *In:* BASSANEZI, Carla (org.); PEDRO, Joana Maria. **New History of Women in Brazil**. Sao Paulo: Contexto, 2012.

RAGO, Luzia Margareth; MOREIRA, Eduardo F. P. **O que e taylorismo.** Sao Paulo: Brasiliense, 2003.

SCALZO, Marilia. **Magazine journalism**. 3. ed. 2ª reprint. Sao Paulo: Contexto, 2009.

SILVA, Joao Luiz Maximoda.**Transformagoes no espago domestico** - o fogao e a cozinha paulistana, 1870-1930. Annals of the Paulista Museum. Sao Paulo. N. Ser. v. 15 n.2. p. 197-220, Jul.-Dec. 2007.

SILVA FILHO, Antonio Luiz Macedo e. **Between the wire and the grid**: electricity in the daily life of Fortaleza (1945-1965). 2008. Thesis (Doctorate in History) - Pontifical Catholic University of Sao Paulo, Sao Paulo, 2008.

SILVA FILHO, Antonio Luiz Macedo. **Technique and material culture in the city of Fortaleza (1945-1965)**. Projeto Historia (PUCSP), v. 40, p. 293317, 2010.

Printed by Books on Demand GmbH, Norderstedt / Germany